Mineral Whisper

poems by

Z.G. Tomaszewski

Finishing Line Press
Georgetown, Kentucky

Mineral Whisper

ACKNOWLEDGMENTS

Thanks to the editors of these magazines, in which a catch of these poems first
appeared:

Coal Hill Review: "As of a Bird Yet Unidentified"
Crannog Literary Magazine: "Mineral Whisper"
The Moth Magazine: "Fitzpatrick's Boarder"
The SHOp: "Dream of a Past Lover" and "Whiskey Tractor"
Southword Journal: "Soon You Will Be Pollen" (previously titled "Revolution")
The Stony Thursday Book: "Turkeys in the Dirt" and "Aphrodite"

Publisher: Leah Maines

Editor: Christen Kincaid

Cover Art: Z.G. Tomaszewski

Author Photo: Hayley Hungerford

Cover Design: Elizabeth Maines

Printed in the USA on acid-free paper.
Order online: www.finishinglinepress.com
             also available on amazon.com

Author inquiries and mail orders:
Finishing Line Press
P. O. Box 1626
Georgetown, Kentucky 40324
U. S. A.

Table of Contents

As reliable as anything you will ever know,
time moves its dim, heavy thumb over the shoreline
making its changes, its whimsical variations.
Yes, yes, the body never gets away from the world,
its endless granular shuffle and exchange—

everything is one, sooner or later—

Mary Oliver
"Riprap," *The Leaf and the Cloud*

Mineral Whisper

The wind off the ocean
        breathes on the cliffs with a mineral whisper
                I sit on the shore listening

In my palm are stone
        and water molecules
                Speak the syllables short and slow

My body is Braille to wind
        I am an oar staked in soil
                A stenciled light on water

and my shadow is greeted by the shades
        of the tree's veined leaves
                I am bewitched

embraced by and embracing the erosion of bone
        a map gaining legend
                Sensations of

fragile light
        Morning sun's sap
                Throughout the day I collect

fields of throat-calls meadows of vowels
        the cliffs' hard consonants
                O but what contains me

The captive sun climbs from its
        fugitive clouds
                an orb of flint striking cliffs

Tides spark as they slap shore
        River takes the name of land
                and runs with it out to ocean

There's a world in each of us
        and mine tends toward wholeness
           and simplicity

The pale tin moon loosens
        from the webbing of stars: an insect
           in a constellation of gossamer

I am pulled by two bodies of light
        such as water
           I inhale to buoy exhale to sink

The scale always in measure
        mineral whisper echoes:
           Where not that this

Aphrodite

When their dorsal fins divide air for an ascending instant
I feel a wind leave my lungs and sweep the waterskin
like the lighthouse's beam exhaling to sea.

Where Carrigaholt Beach overlaps Rinevalla Bay
a lone boat motors by—a swift melancholy.
I will see the skipper later in town and ask him

about the catch: "A beauty she was, lad, a resistant one too,
she had half a mind not to be landed—" his eyebrows raised
like mackerel mid jump, their arc frozen.

He bobs his head with a tug and reel of a pole, its line
dragged in from the depths. As I have cast for you.
I am wanting to reel, to bring you closer, but I am afraid the line

will snap if I try too hard, if I turn too quick. There's no hook,
nothing sharp. For now I only want to hold you in my hands
so I may better know how to hold you in my eyes.

The skipper tucks talk in his pocket and steps away.
The sky thickens. And I wonder if I should slacken the line.
I recognize your wariness.

Dream of a Past Lover

Last night I dreamt of a former
lover. We shared the bed and each other
all evening. The bed a boat
and our arms oar's
we rowed the Shannon Estuary,
as I was rowing in her. The clouds
balloons ascending from a field.
It was a hopeful abandonment, she confided,
waves rocking the bed,
light paddling through a sea of clouds—
the wind released and the rhythm of
our breathing broken. She turned from me
after a mermaid's kiss, lifting her arms
back into the boat; I rowed until water calmed
then rolled my body to hers
after an unraveling that even sailor's desire.
Like two sea creatures washed ashore,
our bodies curving unison, drying out.
Her smiling and, before I woke, swimming away.

Leaning Into the Siren

Half-tuned wind chimes
in the shape of spires
built from the tusks of narwhales.

A captain completely drunk
on someone's porch steps, sad
about his sunken ship, wobbles
to his feet, holding the intoxicating sea
in a bottle between his hands.
The sidewalk a janky plank,
a long haul off keel, land uncharted,
an unfamiliar sound, leaning into the siren.
No life preserver, no vest of buoys,
just a braid of hair and a single notion:
a feather rewinding to its nest,
his vessel rocking in the ocean's hands,
brought down to bed, and a sudden
wave—the wind enlivening the narwhale
and a tower of half-pitched letting-gos.

Shelley, a Swan, and the Storm

On his white boat that sails like a swan
        over the iron-lunged ocean he hears
                the howling cloud and sees it swell—

the clay-colored air like charcoal smoke
        stirred by the swan's gray
                webbed feet and its wings white oars

paddling off the slate-blue water—
        all that elaborate effort
                and the raging heart of

the storm, the terror within man—the swan
        lifts away from the chain of waves
                drifting unmoored

Fishermen

One week they snag a starfish, the next a line of mackerel. "De most beautiful fish you'll ever land," said one as I approached. O yes, I've seen it, the body of miniscule bones and scales like a mandala. I blew but the pattern remained, the colors kept deeper than flesh; my breath became visible, morphed into granules of sand, scattered, each grain a small stone skipping through air. The fishermen saw, looked at me, and with little amusement said, "Still not as stunnin' as a catch of mackerel, which can be eat'n. What's yer lot, lad? Think yer a saint? You'll go hungry like all de rest... Tis a pity when youngens like yerself starve kuss yer world is all odd fancy." I was without reply, lightened and lifted and darkened and grounded. When I inhaled, the line of both poles tightened, each with an ornament of fish. The men bothered a nod, held the fish, fingers hooked under gills, heads facing sky, drinking the sun. I hadn't the faintest what came over me, and the fishermen: disenchanted. They'd spear a god if they could. But the cliffs from where they stand are still too far from the source. Me? I'll build a raft of bones with a sail of scales. I'll call upon the mackerel to keep me afloat, I'll slurp the salty stalks of kelp—all so I am closer than the fishermen to the center. And after, I'll come back biting.

Black-Crowned Night

Because I'm a black-crowned night heron I can kill.
My weapon is yellow-sharp—

I stab at water, scab the scales of fish. I hunt in hiding.
My disguise: stillness—blending black feathers with
       shadow-soaked trees.

I wait to wield my shovel-mouth sword.
I don't want a scoop of sand, I want the slippery arc

of swimming muscle, I want meat—
a body throbbing with energy.

This is the pull that quickens my pulse, that leads me
into your sight, that threatens survival.

Eyes of Holy Water

Like osmosis I will enter your skin
through rain and seep in to cool
your burning spirit
but first you must lick the ring of your lips
and feel the pearls of misted dust
then taste the chill of clouds
their condensation abbreviated
on the purse of another's mouth
so when you feel the trickle of truth
look out with your eyes of holy water
and baptize the toad below you
quivering before it croaks

As of a Bird Yet Unidentified

The sea carves at sand
a sculpture engrained with salt
and peppered by the pitch
of wind.

Clouds balloon over water
under the mirror
sweeps a tango of fish.

I swim
at the place the plane the point
where water touches air
at the interstice of oxygen
the distance between body and body.

When it comes to the spirit
what is
ordinary?

I suppose sparrow bones
and finch feathers

not the eyes
of an oriole
the one I saw threading
a thatched teardrop-shaped house
an inverted haystack
where lay two more worlds.

The bird-mother's pupils streak and stain the shells.

That thin membrane
then the storm
the sky's slate shadow
like a tightly-stitched suit.

How I was no longer
convinced that I wanted
wings

so donning my human hide
I stepped out into the nest of the storm
to see
how elastic of an egg
I am.

Spring

the storm's black
jacket shoulders over
sun but from its holed
pockets light spills out
laces of lightning
unravel and with it
thunder threads through
to the boots your grandpa
gave you now a cloud
covering your cold feet
that buoy you as you
slosh through the bay
of rain on your way
to his grave the sky with
nothing more to give

Fitzpatrick's Boarder

The pubman tells a story of a boarder
while the jolly man laughs,
his stomach bouncing up and down; his friend,
in vest and spectacles, holds right hand to chin
as if studying it—*Madmen!*
the boarder from the story shouts, pointing
to the crows above the apartment. She claims
they wouldn't leave her alone, that they sat outside
the window smoking cigarettes, flicking
feathers and ash against the glass.
(The ceiling-sky begins to brown.)
"At least the crows kept it outside," chortles the jolly man
like a clown with a balloon on his lap.
The pubman smiles, says, "No such thing," then continues:
"She said she'd rather be *a scarecrow in a field
than a prisoner in this public house.*" He pauses,
adjusts the fist on his hip, "She was cuckoo,
a few bits loose upstairs, the clock always alarmed,
know what I mean? Odd thing is," he adds,
"when she went the crows kept coming around
painting my building with their shit, dammit.
And the room she was in is still filled
with a gauze of smoke. She wasn't even a smoker!"
The jolly man misses a laugh, his studious friend
scratches the skin under cap; lights flicker,
a floorboard squawks, silence flies into the room.

Whiskey Tractor
for J.J. McMahon

I knock on his door at nine o'clock.
A current kicks in, shuffle of feet, the door
opens with a questioning creak.
     He scans my scarecrow appearance with
his weathered eyes. He invites me in and
immediately assumes the seat he rose from.
"I'm just eating breakfast, go on take a chair."
The knife in his calloused hand cuts dimension
into the butter, covers the bread like topsoil,
a slant of Pantry jam angled atop, raspberry
seeds pimpled in the sweetness, a flag of ham
laid down and between two leathery fingers
the bulb of a tomato. A pot of Barry's tea and
a bottle of Jameson keep him company.
He offers a drink and I accept.
     A heavy tipping, last night the sky
poured too many stars in his cup; he drank
a constellation. So as he steps out and sees
the sun, not rising in the east as he might expect
but staggering in the west, he remarks:
"Well, I guess the Earth is off her rocker."
     A couple tugs more and we're on our way
to count cattle. The latch on the tractor door is
whack, but we manage, both of us aboard and
soon we're being carried north up the hill on
the scraped-paint tractor cough- and sputtering.
     The sun hiccups and is swallowed
beyond the horizon. Exhaust smoke
becoming clouds in the sky.
     J.J. is humming (Martin Hayes maybe?),
his mouth motoring, the diseased harmonies
of the machine muffling the tune, concerting
an original engine song. I inhale, fill
my lungs with an ocean of Atlantic air and
form lips like two cliffs at Dunlicky
coming to point pinching wind, and I whistle…
the whiskey tractor a-reeling.

The March

Past hedge-crowned chassis that could've been my grandfather's,
past huge tools for a trade rusted away, on a well-trodden path of
gravel hoof-ground to dirt, the cattle march once in the yawn
of morn and again at the flute of dusk, downhill south
to the stalls where warm hands grasp the chime of cool udders
tug and sound horn: milk-splashing rhythm against tin;

where the farmer with his three-legged stool is seated: a busker
plays an instrument: it's the song of dairy cows that continues
after the milking when they march uphill north past
the refuse-now-artifacts to the far field where they're free—
grazing jaw thumps, the pasture humming with hoof-fall
and wind buzzing like a bee through an open hive.

Call it Carmody's Field. Consider your life. Take a walk one day
to see for yourself what shape the light takes beyond the rise.
Share in the cattle's view of the Atlantic swelling and subsuming,
but motionless all the while. Stay there in the field all afternoon;
be at pasture. Consider your life. And when you must move,
do so without haste. There's no hurry here.

When the time of the sky signals with its sidelight from the west
make the march back with the cattle and examine the slant sun
behind you; as you reach the pen separate to stretch for a stool,
slap rope around waist, tie to the stool, and take seat—imagine
Sonny beside you showing his son Damien the milking man's grip,
feel in your hands the vitality and necessity of the cow's life force.

And whistle: for a string of notes keeps them from wanting to kick
the pail. Recall the pasture of the Atlantic. Remember the wind
lift- and tasseling the feed grass. Remember the march. Whistle
now, keep to it. This is how you know the work is meaningful.

Soon You Will Be Pollen

Take a clip of sun and turn it,
        twist and stretch and lay it across the meadow.

See the bee? Grab it. Then let go
        in the strong wind you make from your mouth.

Twirl the clouds around your arm,
        when the white gauze reaches shoulder: shake

and extend and watch
        as it sails like pollen after the bumble-drunk bee.

The creek, call towards it. Speak
        its name, you know it, you do, it's inside you.

Quiet. Wait for it. The echo.
        Return to the sun, clench a grain and again stretch

but this time cast it over the creekbed.
        Lay down. Let the bee come back to you, it will.

Wait. Quiet. The clouds, can you hear
        their whisper? They're saying your name, asking

for you. Quiet. Wait. Return. Return
        to what you were doing before stumbling upon this.

Turkeys in the Dirt

          stir up dust, a tornado
bath on the naked skirt of grass.
I'm beyond the hem, deep in the bog,
barely visible.

I note nine in numbers, some young
neck to neck with their mothers—
O to have your tenderness
          your warmth needed.

They flap wide
blacken-brown harped wings
carving apparitions in the wind,
scoop into dirt hearth
for heat—this (can you believe?)
is what cleans them.

          O consider me clean
if I rise out of a marsh swamp-scented
mud-clothed and muck-faced
carrying the warm musk
of Earth's dark blood
          under my boots.

What Survives of an Old Stone Wall

Moss. A few gray slabs sunk in the ground.
Surely not the man whose hands remember
the cold, jagged edges, the density of Earth's
matter, the dirt ridged under his nails, but
the story, passed through generations, told
to those who will hear it, who will put their
soft ears to the hard stone. Those who know
the trade would recognize that wall, would
know of the man whose shoulders carried
the weight of a world. And anyone building
his own wall could learn a thing or two from
the hermit who attempted to secure his seclusion:

Walls falling, Earth reclaiming what it will.

Bus Ride in Ireland with Paul Muldoon and Stanley Kunitz

The bus driver is a young Paul Muldoon.
The bus: his instrument to map the road.

Seated in front of me: a woman whose eyelashes
have more curl than the fold of a white-cap.

I swear that's Stanley Kunitz across the aisle:
thick but trimmed moustache—a cloud above
his lips at the basin of those cheekbones, his nose

with a similar width and slope; a cap made of wool
with a loose button top center.

I return to reading. The bus traces a roundabout,
wheels circling: primary, secondary, mixing.

We pass post office/pubs, dash through those
small towns surrounded by bog
where a *rolling fog* is swallowed then hiccupped.

We're carried on a land-boat, Muldoon
humming a tune, turning the wheel like an image in his head.

I look out the window as we motor on:
greens swirl and blend to shifting sea-blues

while loud white engines of clouds tangle
in the brown/gray of thickets.
Beyond the man who resembles Stanley, passing

through the frame, I see a lone boat tracking water.
The rising rhythms and waves of

words from "The Long Boat" recur:
To be rocked by the Infinite!

The woman ahead of me glances back,
looks beyond to something distant in her past.

The bus rolls on with its catalytic rattle,
as if it didn't matter/ which way was home.

Visiting Seamus Heaney

I knock, knuckling the wood of at least a dozen doors. The ridges
on my left hand's middle knuckles worn, calluses forming like
miniature cabbage heads. All the while I'm on the way I imagine
our conversation: 'The gentle hand of Aeolus has guided me
accordingly, a few spirals of confusion and breezy encounters but
no bother.' From bus to train and plenty of walking, fragments of a
dialogue: 'Just yesterday,' I say. (Seamus scans my stained clothes.) 'I
was cleaning stables, pitching manure for topsoil and chasing eight
horses from one field across the road to another.' I'll mention the
forty cattle P.J. Roche and I had to guide from pasture to pasture
and bring up the well on the latter pasture where an eel still shapes
the base. I'll ask him about saints and ceremonious wells and he'll
respond— St. Brigid and St. Kevin—then speak seamlessly among
various reminiscences: bricklayers, blackbirds, a sofa in the forties,
his rough voice softening as he recalls "sunstruck pendulums" and
"the poplar." Maybe I'll invoke: 'Incline, as an elder, the slow speech of
a sycamore, the studded skin of spuds—how the dirt in those divots
grounds under one's nails as they're scratched before the stew. Incline
the tide with the smoke from the ash plant stacks riding their backs,
translate that myth for me; or the molting swans or the flotsam.' It's
a thick door that absorbs the clamber of an earnest hand after the
knock reverberates through the front room—the door a casket slat
trapping guest-tapped echoes. So much history held in its grooves—
like a spade handle: connected to those who have come before. His
dame answers, unlatches the lock, swings the door to a 45 degree
angle, an exact slant that permits enough openness without yielding
privacy. She ushers him out, a curiosity framed in the entryway. In
minutes the anticipation that coursed through me like seeds trickling
in a hollow stick is washed away: he is not able to talk long since the
children and grandchildren are there and the table set for a family
feast. (What food would be consumed? Damsons? Steamed leeks with
bread and butter and fallen columns of pollock or cod?). He stands,
not leaning against the jamb, but with a stance that perpetuates my
flight path. I amble off along Sandymount Strand—"rock-lover, loner,
sky-sentry," having hailed and heading home.

Plane in a Smaller Plane

The sky is a mattress
comprised of thousands of
invisibly threaded
satin clouds. If you were
to view it from above:
a carpet of wool, and
at dusk, due to the arc
of Earth and how Sun slides
down, the effervescent
ceiling is a far-reach
purple. The ground gathers
evening hues, matching
itself to the mask of
midnight. White unravels
into blackberry-June.
A firefly the lone light
in Atlantic's backyard.

Astral Eyes

Far from sea I watch the waves
of sky: cloud-tide of cirrus
sweeping to the distant shore
of outer space—grains of stardust
like stones dancing in an ocean.
I reach for
but cannot touch. Beyond my body
the spirit seeks a meadow of coral.
Bulbs of the celestial comet-flower
blinding with energy—
a galaxy strewn with seaweed.

Bury me here in skyweed,
cerulean and sapphire
streaked by the emerald of asteroids.

Let rain begin,
the liquid rocks splashing
like meteors skipped across welkin waters.

Listening to Van Morrison While in Moveen, Ireland

At the cottage, which was for a long time Nora Lynch's, there was a Van Morrison mixtape and a small CD player with a knack for skipping, as if the music excited it to dance. So that's what I began to do. I wasn't alone. I was dancing with Aphrodite to the tune of "Beside You," with Nora for a moment Madame George: the sweet perfume now cigarette smoke covering her shoulders like a wool shawl. In a tobacco fog I imagined her and me *breathing in and breathing out and breathing in and breathing out* until *we walked away from it all...so calm.* By "Spanish Rose" we were eating soup. The guitar took me from the table to a street where bulls run—then the track changed and I *stumbled on a crack* on my way back to the stone cottage. Inside I reached for a drink of water and sat to finish the food—cabbage folded onto the spoon like a sheet on the line. I could see past Carmody's Field: the Atlantic. I could hear the faint opening chords of "Astral Weeks"—when the notes fade, the fields reappear and we are in the "Back Room." From there it's a *hillside retreating view:* where cattle march daily between the borders of their lots, lives framed by berms and stone walls and the ever-pressing arc of the horizon. The horizon: a rising tenor sax with the sky a symphony of altocumulus. I'm struggling to make music here—plucking order out of chaos—still that's what music is: sound strummed out of silence. *Sometimes I'm overcome thinking about it.* So I just hum: *Sha la la la la la la la la lala de dah*

Coda

I stood there my whole life
I was nowhere
          else and I was everywhere
in the mineral whisper

NOTES

This book, in part, is for Thomas Lynch. Your far-reaching generosity deserves more than a dedication. Alas, I will help stock the turf shed again, and write a few new poems in the ledger.

For the rest of this life I am grateful to P.J. Roche for bringing me into the thick and endless pastures, time and misted time again. One day I will write a poem about your father and his horses. Until then, keeping whispering.

My gratitude to those early readers and enthusiasts of this book before it was a book. A great breath of thanks especially, Kyle Vandeventer.

Also, for keen editorial suggestions on this manuscript, sweeping thanks to Phillip Sterling.

Patricia Clark, Chris Dombrowski, and Rodney Torreson are in good standing as well.

I am grateful to Gina and Tim Gort for our friendship and for the letters we had during the slow unfolding of this manuscript.

"Whiskey Tractor" is for J.J. McMahon (and the tweed hat he gave me). In the poem, Martin Hayes is mentioned, he is an exemplary Irish fiddler.

The quoted passages in "Bus Ride in Ireland with Paul Muldoon and Stanley Kunitz" are from Stanley Kunitz's poem "The Long Boat."

Lines and phrases in "Visiting Seamus Heaney" are borrowed out of his book *The Spirit Level*.

"As of a Bird Yet Unidentified" was written while reading Joshua Poteat's *Ornithologies*.

After a series of ramblings and residencies in Ireland and Vermont and hitch-hiking out west, culminating in a job at Glacier National Park, Montana, **Z.G. Tomaszewski**, born in 1989, lives in Grand Rapids where he aspires to fish the river every morning and play bossa nova in a lounge by night. For now, Tomaszewski works maintenance at an old Masonic Temple and is a founding member and events coordinator of Great Lakes Commonwealth of Letters and co-director of Lamp Light Music Festival. His debut book *All Things Dusk* was the winner of the International Poetry Prize of 2014, chosen by Li-Young Lee, and published by Hong Kong University Press.

www.ingramcontent.com/pod-product-compliance
Lightning Source LLC
LaVergne TN
LVHW021124080426
835510LV00021B/3310